NORTHBROOK PUBLIC LIBRARY
1201 CEDAR LANE
NORTHBROOK, ILL 60062

JUN 0 2 2016

P9-BZB-633

Northbrook Public Library

DISCARDED

3 1123 01133 3872

GENETIC CONDITIONS

Huntington's Disease

RANDALL MCPARTLAND

Cavendish Square

New York

Published in 2016 by Cavendish Square Publishing, LLC
243 5th Avenue, Suite 136, New York, NY 10016

Copyright © 2016 by Cavendish Square Publishing, LLC

First Edition

No part of this publication may be reproduced, stored in a retrieval system, or transmitted in any form or by any means—electronic, mechanical, photocopying, recording, or otherwise—without the prior permission of the copyright owner. Request for permission should be addressed to Permissions, Cavendish Square Publishing, 243 5th Avenue, Suite 136, New York, NY 10016. Tel (877) 980-4450; fax (877) 980-4454.

Website: cavendishsq.com

This publication represents the opinions and views of the author based on his or her personal experience, knowledge, and research. The information in this book serves as a general guide only. The author and publisher have used their best efforts in preparing this book and disclaim liability rising directly or indirectly from the use and application of this book.

CPSIA Compliance Information: Batch #CW16CSQ

All websites were available and accurate when this book was sent to press.

Cataloging-in-Publication Data

McPartland, Randall.
Huntington's disease / by Randall McPartland.
p. cm. — (Genetic conditions)
Includes index.
ISBN 978-1-5026-0942-7 (hardcover) ISBN 978-1-5026-0943-4 (ebook)
1. Huntington's disease — Juvenile literature. I. McPartland, Randall. II. Title.
RC394.H85 M39 2016
616.8'3—d23

Editorial Director: David McNamara
Editor: Fletcher Doyle
Copy Editor: Nathan Heidelberger
Art Director: Jeffrey Talbot
Designer: Alan Sliwinski
Senior Production Manager: Jennifer Ryder-Talbot
Production Editor: Renni Johnson
Photo Research: J8 Media

The photographs in this book are used by permission and through the courtesy of: Stefano Lunardi/Shutterstock.com, cover; AP Photo/The Country Today, Paul M. Walsh, 5; AP Photo/Bob Child, 8; Dani Carlo/Prisma Bildagentur AG/Alamy, 10; BSIP/UIG via Getty Images, 12; B Lamb/Shutterstock.com, 15; Bibliotheque de la Faculte de Medecine, Paris, France/Archives Charmet/Bridgeman Images, 18; Iculig/Shutterstock.com, 20; Atulji/Shutterstock.com, 23; Photo Researchers, 26; AP Photo/Lowell Sun/Robert Whitaker, 29; AP Photo/Damian Dovarganes, 32; Vasin Lee/Shutterstock.com, 35; Mint Images/Getty Images, 37; Conor Caffrey/Science Source, 39; Seth Joel/Photographer's Choice/Getty Images, 40; By The Hayden family (Original photograph) [Public domain], via Wikimedia Commons, 46; Biophoto Associates/Science Source, 48; Toshifumi Kitamura/AFP/Getty Images, 50; Laguna Design/Getty Images, 54.

Printed in the United States of America

CONTENTS

INTRODUCTION

Discovering that one of your parents has Huntington's disease delivers a double blow. Not only will you find out your parent will slowly deteriorate in the next few decades, you will also learn that you have a 50 percent chance of developing a fatal disease. This is a scenario faced by an estimated two hundred thousand people in the United States.

Huntington's disease (HD) causes nerve cells in certain areas of the brain to deteriorate. As this happens, it becomes harder to control thoughts, feelings, and movements. Eventually, the body becomes too weak to fight off other illnesses, leading to death. Infections, such as pneumonia, are the most common causes of death. After a person first begins to develop symptoms of HD, he or she will usually live between ten and thirty more years.

HD is a **genetic** disease, meaning a person inherits the disease from a parent. How do people know if they're at risk of developing HD? First, a person has to know if either of his or her biological (birth) parents has HD. If the answer is yes,

Shana Martin Verstegen is a world champion in log rolling and boom running. She has not been tested for Huntington's disease, which killed her mother.

special blood tests can determine if that person has the defective gene that causes HD.

The early symptoms of HD vary from person to person. Physical, or "movement," symptoms can include mild clumsiness and muscle spasms. As the disease progresses, these symptoms increase. People with HD may also have trouble with their speech. For example, people with HD may notice that their speech becomes halting or slurred as the disease progresses. Some people with HD also have trouble swallowing.

HD symptoms also include emotional and cognitive problems, or difficulties involving thought and memory. For example, a person may have trouble learning new things or keeping information straight. Over time, it may become harder and harder to remember or to pay attention. Many people with HD also experience depression and mood swings.

Researchers are getting closer to understanding exactly what happens in a person to bring on HD. With that knowledge, they may be able to find a cure for the disease. When that happens, a diagnosis of Huntington's disease will no longer be doubly devastating.

Chapter One

Gene Hunting

Great advances in medical science are often driven by the passion of a few people. The force that led to much of what has been learned about Huntington's disease was a family's love for Leonore Wexler, a wife and mother.

Leonore Wexler was diagnosed with HD in 1968. Milton Wexler was devastated by his wife's disease and was determined to learn more. He and his two daughters, Nancy and Alice, embarked on a search for a cure. Milton Wexler was a well-known psychologist. He worked hard to bring together world-renowned researchers to focus on HD research. He established the Foundation for Research in **Hereditary** Disease, which later became the Hereditary Disease Foundation. The foundation funds research and sponsors workshops where researchers can share information and ideas about HD.

Nancy Wexler and Supreme Court justice Sandra Day O'Connor received honorary degrees from Yale in 2006.

Nancy Wexler, who graduated from Radcliffe the year before her mother's diagnosis and earned a PhD in clinical psychology in 1974, played a key role in HD research as well. Leonore Wexler died in 1978, and the next year her daughter became a gene hunter. Backed by the foundation started by her father, she led a team of scientists to Lake Maracaibo in Venezuela to study an unusually dense cluster of HD patients who live there.

Huntington's disease is a genetic disorder in which the nerve cells of the brain break down over a period of years. It is always fatal, but people can live ten to thirty years after they are diagnosed. Some patients lose up to 25 percent of their brain cells before they die. Among the symptoms are an unsteady gait, involuntary and uncontrollable movements, personality changes, mood swings, depression, forgetfulness, slurred speech, impaired judgment, difficulty in swallowing, and significant weight loss.

The disease is passed on in an autosomal **dominant** fashion. Autosomal means the gene responsible for the disease is not located on either of the sex **chromosomes**, known as the X and Y chromosomes, that determine the sex of the person. Therefore the disease afflicts males and females equally. The condition is dominant, so a child needs to inherit just one copy of the gene, from either his or her mother or father, to get the disease. The child of a parent with HD has a 50 percent chance of inheriting the disease. In contrast, conditions caused by recessive genes require that the child inherit that gene from both parents. Cystic fibrosis (CF) is a recessive condition. A person with one CF gene will not get the disease but will be a carrier for the disease. If two carriers have a child, that child will have a 25 percent chance of inheriting the disease.

Breakthrough

In 2004, Nancy Wexler and the United States–Venezuela Collaborative Research Project show that the age at which a person begins to show signs of HD is not determined by the Huntington gene alone. Instead, the age of onset is strongly influenced by genes other than the Huntington gene, as well as by environmental factors.

Dominant conditions show up in more family members than recessive conditions do. Nancy Wexler lost not only her mother, but also a grandfather and three uncles to Huntington's disease.

The three villages around Lake Maracaibo are isolated and don't experience a lot of turnover in the families that live there. The families there that carry the gene continue to pass it down through generations, creating a concentration of people affected by the defective gene. This gives HD researchers a large group of people to study in one area.

In 1979, Nancy Wexler made her first of many annual trips to the region to collect family histories and skin and blood samples of people with the disease.

Remote villages on Lake Maracaibo in Venezuela provide controlled conditions for the study of Huntington's disease.

Researchers James Gusella, Michael Conneally, and David Housman looked at the **DNA** of the affected people, trying to see what they had in common. Their work paid quick dividends even though the technology available to researchers was crude by today's standards. Researchers had to analyze these samples one by one, using bacterial **enzymes** to cut up the DNA they collected. In contrast, by 2007, robotic machines could analyze a half million samples at a time.

Dr. Wexler's samples helped lead to the discovery of a genetic marker for HD in 1983. Genetic markers are sequences of DNA with a known location on a chromosome. Sequences of DNA tend to be inherited, so these markers can be used to link an inherited disease with the responsible gene. These markers appeared on chromosome 4 of people with Huntington's disease, so the search for the faulty gene started there.

LETTERS OF GENETIC LAWS

Whether a person will develop HD depends on his or her DNA. DNA stands for deoxyribonucleic acid. Humans and other living organisms pass information to their offspring through DNA. When two people have a baby, DNA from each parent is the key ingredient passed on to the baby. It determines the baby's eye and hair color, skin color, and more. DNA can also carry some unwanted traits, however, including genetic diseases like HD.

One helpful way to understand DNA is to think about the English-language alphabet. We use twenty-six letters to form words. We then use these words to make sentences, which in turn help us to communicate. DNA has its own four-letter alphabet, or chemical code: A, C, G, and T. These are called

nucleotides, and each one represents a chemical, or base. Here is what the letters stand for:

A = adenine

C = cytosine

G = guanine

T = thymine

In the English language, words can be made up of just a few letters or many letters, but DNA words, or codes, are more

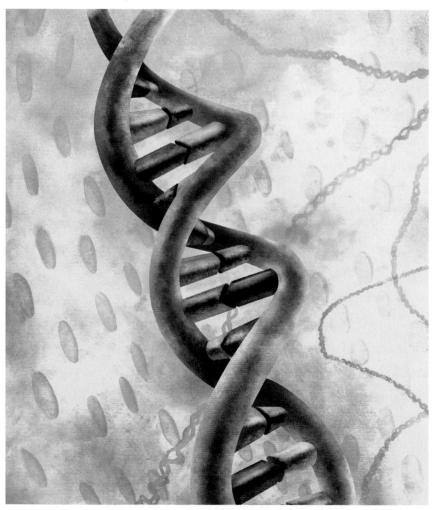

In a double helix of DNA, the same bases–adenine to thymine and cytosine to guanine–always pair up.

Huntington's Disease

uniform, with specific rules for how the letters are arranged. For example, A always pairs with T, and C always pairs with G. If you were to look at a DNA molecule, you would see what looks like a long, twisting ladder. This is called a double helix. Each "rung" of the ladder is made up of two paired nucleotide bases. Combinations of these pairs create a code that determines a gene's function. Human bodies have approximately twenty-five thousand genes, and each of these genes provides information that contributes to an individual's characteristics.

So, a gene is a long string of DNA, and the gene's function depends on the sequence of nucleotide bases in the DNA. For scientists researching Huntington's disease, identifying the Huntington gene brought them one very large step closer to understanding the disease.

THE HUNTINGTON GENE

Our genes are arranged in very precise locations along twenty-three rodlike pairs of chromosomes. One chromosome from each pair comes from our mother. The other comes from our father. By gene standards, the Huntington gene is quite long, with more than three hundred thousand nucleotide base pairs. Sequences of three nucleotide bases are called codons. Each codon is a DNA instruction telling the cell to produce a certain amino acid. In humans, there are twenty amino acids that link together in a series to make **proteins**. One of these amino acids, **glutamine,** is coded for by the codon C-A-G (or CAG).

Nancy Wexler and her researchers looked for an error in the genetic code on chromosome 4 because they thought that would be the source of Huntington's disease. Their search ended after

Family Secret

One of the great tools for predicting Huntington's disease is a family history. If the disease runs in a family, members can be monitored for symptoms and treatment can begin quickly. Early treatment can slow the advance of the disease and increase the patient's quality of life.

The involuntary movements, paranoia, and emotional outbursts that are characteristics of people with HD can be unsettling to others. Before the disease was discovered, people with it were shunned or were thought to be either witches or possessed by evil spirits.

In the sixteenth century, physician and **alchemist** Paracelsus (1493–1541) coined the term **chorea** to describe the frenzied movements of religious fanatics who visited the healing shrine of St. Vitus during the middle ages.

In the 1630s, English colonists in Massachusetts used the term "Saint Vitus's dance" to describe the type of movement we now associated with HD. St. Vitus's Dance, also known as Sydenham's chorea, can cause a dancing mania. In 1692, many people were accused of being possessed by the devil because of their uncontrolled body movements. About twenty were tried and sentenced to death in the famous witch trials in Salem, Massachusetts. Some historians now believe some of these people may have had HD.

Later on, people with HD were placed in institutions and kept a family secret. Now we know it's best to get information on HD out in the open.

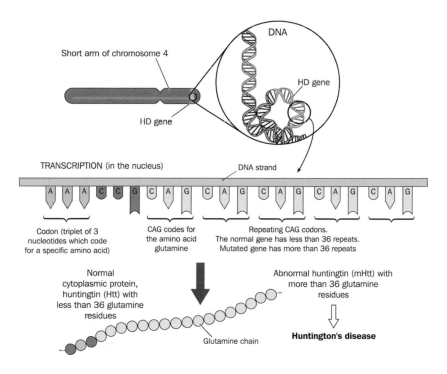

The Huntington gene is found on the short arm of chromosome 4. A codon of CAG codes for the amino acid glutamine. Chains of amino acids form proteins. In a healthy Huntington gene, the chain of glutamine contains no more than thirty-six repeats of the CAG codon. A chain with forty or more repeats causes Huntington's disease.

eight long years, aided greatly by a discovery made by someone else. Albert La Spada, then a doctoral candidate at the University of Pennsylvania, found that **genetic mutations** could be caused by a stutter and not an error in the code. He found a genetic disease that was caused by the repetition of a correct code too many times. Wexler's researchers confirmed that this stutter was present in people with HD.

In a normal Huntington gene, there is a section in which the CAG codon is repeated up to thirty-six times. In a defective Huntington gene, however, the CAG codon repeats more than forty times. This means that for people with HD, there are too many glutamines produced by the Huntington gene. When there are too many glutamines, the **huntingtin** protein molecules stick together and form into tangled, rigid groups that are called protein **aggregates**. When these aggregates build up, they get in the way of normal nerve cell function. This brings about nerve cell dysfunction and death. Huntington's disease belongs in a group known as trinucleotide repeat disorders. These are a set of genetic disorders in which a segment of DNA that contains a repeat of three nucleotides (CAG in this case) expands so there are more of the repeats than are needed. Slippage during DNA replication causes triplet expansion.

Nancy Wexler also helped researchers map genes responsible for other diseases, including Alzheimer's disease, kidney cancer, and certain mental disorders. Her work on locating the genetic marker for Huntington's disease is credited with getting others to push for the Human **Genome** Project.

As of 2015, Nancy Wexler was the president of the Hereditary Disease Foundation.

Chapter Two

A Long Search

Scientists had been looking for answers to the mystery of Huntington's disease long before the family of Leonore Wexler got involved. Symptoms of Huntington's disease have been written about for a long time.

It wasn't until the 1840s that HD was first described in medical literature as "chronic hereditary chorea." At this time, three doctors—one in the United States, one in England, and one in Norway—each described, in separate accounts, the involuntary movements and mental disturbances of their patients. They also noted that these traits appeared to be inherited from a parent who displayed similar behavior. But the cause of HD and how to treat it remained a mystery.

Finally, in 1872, a famous paper called "On Chorea" was published in the United States in the Philadelphia journal

This lithograph from the early nineteenth century shows people dancing wildly in front of a statue of St. Vitus to obtain a year of good health. The dance became confused with chorea.

the *Medical and Surgical Reporter*. The paper was written by George Huntington. Huntington was an American doctor who described the symptoms of chorea in detail. Huntington based his paper on notes he took while observing his father's and grandfather's patients. Both men were doctors who had noticed involuntary shaking in some of their patients. Huntington described how these symptoms were common in families, and he believed that the disease was inherited. In addition to physical symptoms, Huntington also noted the patients' mental decline. The careful observations and conclusions outlined in Huntington's paper helped spark widespread interest in the disease, which was eventually named after him.

It took many more years of research, however, before scientists were able to figure out what part of the brain was being affected by the disease. In 1910, researchers finally identified the parts of the brain that are the targets of cell death in patients with HD. These structures are the **caudate nuclei.** (A single one is called a caudate nucleus.)

Another key turning point in the study of HD occurred in 1953, when James Watson and Francis Crick discovered the structure of deoxyribonucleic acid (DNA). DNA is the key to our bodies' genetic makeup. The discovery of its structure came at a time when there was a growing interest in human genetics. Many people accurately believed that learning about DNA was also the key to finding a cure to some genetic diseases. There was a surge in publications about HD, but the disease still remained a puzzling mystery—one that a growing number of people wanted to solve.

Breakthrough

In the 1850s, Gregor Mendel, a monk from Austria, figures out some laws of genetic inheritance by planting lots of varieties of peas in his monastery garden to observe the reproductive patterns of the flowering plants. Mendel discovers that during reproduction, each plant transmits one copy of each gene to its offspring and that each gene pair is inherited independently. He first presents his findings in 1865.

ANNIVERSARY DISCOVERIES

In 1972, on the one hundredth anniversary of the publication of George Huntington's famous paper "On Chorea," HD researchers held the International Centennial Symposium on Huntington's Disease. They got together to collect all the information known about HD up to that date. During that same year, Thomas L. Perry discovered lowered levels of GABA (gamma-aminobutyric acid) in the brains of HD patients. GABA is a hormone that regulates levels of dopamine in the brain. Dopamine is a chemical in the brain that helps regulate movement, balance, and walking. Lower levels of GABA weaken the motor system of the body and lead to the movement symptoms of HD. Many thought this could be a clue to how HD progressed.

Lab rats were studied to observe the progression of symptoms of Huntington's disease.

Huntington's Disease Fact Sheet

» There are about 30,000 people in the United States with HD.

» Symptoms of the disease usually appear in people between the ages of thirty-five and fifty.

» In about 10 percent of cases, symptoms will start in people younger than twenty. This is known as juvenile Huntington's disease (JHD).

» There are about 200,000 people with a 50 percent risk of having HD because they have a parent with the condition.

» The estimated rate of HD in the United States and Europe is 5 cases per 100,000 people. The disease is more rare in other countries such as Japan, where the rate of HD is between 0.1 and 0.38 people per 100,000.

» People live between ten and thirty years after the onset of HD symptoms.

» The disease is caused by forty or more CAG repeats on chromosome 4. People with JHD have a higher number of repeats than those with they typical form of HD.

In 1976, Joseph T. Coyle developed the first rat model of HD. Using rat models allows researchers to study the progression of diseases. Coyle inserted the chemical kainic acid into the brains of rats to cause damage to a specific area of the brain that controls movement, balance, and walking. After the injections, the rats began to exhibit HD-like symptoms including weight loss, uncontrolled movements, and brain damage. By carefully watching the symptoms progress in rats, researchers hoped to learn more about HD and eventually figure out how to control and even prevent its symptoms. The ultimate goal, of course, was to find a cure for HD.

All this research finally led the United States Congress to take action. In 1977, Congress approved the establishment of the Commission for the Control of Huntington's Disease and Its Consequences. The purpose of the commission was to develop a comprehensive report on HD in the United States.

The major breakthrough occurred in 1983, when Wexler and her fellow scientists discovered the gene marker linked to HD. The gene that causes Huntington's disease is called the Huntington gene. Discovering where this gene is located made it possible to figure out how likely it is for a person to inherit HD. Ten years after the general location was discovered, the Huntington gene was located at a more specific site on the chromosome: 4p16.3. This number is the identifier for the Huntington gene. The 4 stands for chromosome 4, the p indicates that it is located on the short arm of the chromosome, and the other numbers pinpoint the exact location on the chromosome where the gene is located. By isolating the gene to this specific location, researchers could then focus on how a defective version of the gene causes HD in the human body.

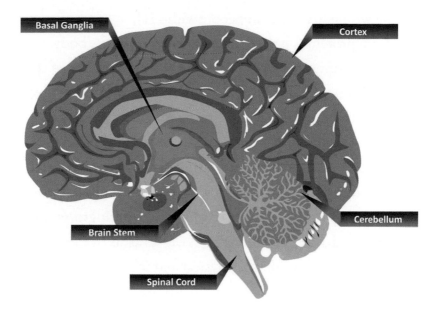

Huntington's disease causes cell death in the neuron-rich basal ganglia, which affects motor movement. Nerve cells communicate when messages are sent from the basal ganglia to the cortex. When nerve cells die in the basal ganglia, the path of these messages is disrupted. One result can be overstimulation of the motor cortex, which may be the reason behind uncontrolled movements.

PROTEIN PROBLEM

The protein produced by the Huntington gene, called the huntingtin protein (Htt), is present in the nerve cells of all humans. Scientists have yet to figure out the exact function of the huntingtin protein, but they do know a lot about it. Huntingtin plays a key role in helping nerve cells function effectively. Scientists also believe that it is necessary for life. In a laboratory, mice that were genetically engineered to lack huntingtin never survived past the embryo stage.

The physical structure of proteins determines how they will function with other parts of the cell. With the huntingtin protein, researchers believe the extra glutamines cause it to have the wrong structure. In people with HD, the defective huntingtin protein is present in cells throughout the body. However, it creates the most problems in the nerve cells of the basal **ganglia**, structures deep in the brain that include the two caudate nuclei. Basal ganglia have many important functions, including coordinating movement.

The faulty huntingtin protein also affects the nerve cells in the brain's outer surface. Called the **cortex**, this part of the brain controls thought, perception, and memory. Huntington's is a **degenerative** disease, meaning that it causes areas of the brain to deteriorate. As a result, the physical and mental functions controlled by these parts of the brain are affected.

Chapter Three

Genetic Time Bomb

The most famous victim of Huntington's disease is the folk singer Woody Guthrie. He was a popular radio entertainer during the 1930s and 1940s. The Oklahoma native became famous for his classic folk songs, including the song "This Land Is Your Land." He wrote in support of the working class, especially those who were adversely affected during the Great Depression.

Guthrie suffered from HD for thirteen years. His mother had suffered similar symptoms, been institutionalized, and died many years earlier. Very little was known about HD then. Before he was finally diagnosed with HD, Guthrie had been misdiagnosed with alcoholism, schizophrenia, and other disorders. He was placed in many different institutions and hospitals for years before he was finally properly diagnosed.

Marjorie Guthrie holds a Conservation Service Award given to a then very ill Woody Guthrie in 1966. Their son Arlo sits between them.

Woody Guthrie died on October 3, 1967, at the age of fifty-five. He was married three times and had a total of eight children. Two of Woody Guthrie's children also died from HD, but his other children are not known to have the disease.

His second wife, Marjorie, established the Committee to Combat Huntington's Disease in 1968, the year Leonore Wexler was diagnosed with the disease. Marjorie Guthrie was one of the people Milton Wexler reached out to when he was trying to drum up support for research.

Singer and a Dancer

Marjorie Guthrie divorced Woody Guthrie when Huntington's disease began to take a toll on him, but she never abandoned him. She told an interviewer in 1977 that the divorce was done so she would not be responsible for paying for his hospitalization.

She cared for their three children, and went with him on his numerous hospital visits. When the famed singer could no longer speak or move his limbs, she taught him to blink his eyes to communicate. After he died in 1967, she worked to draw attention to the disease that killed him.

She founded the Committee to Combat Huntington's Disease, then she raised money to pay to have the first bibliography of articles about the disease published. Her committee identified families in which HD was present. Also, she played a critical role in the creation of the World Federation of **Neurology's** Research Commission on Huntington's Chorea, lectured, and served on many commissions and advisory boards.

Marjorie danced with and then worked for the famous Martha Graham before she married Woody. She died of cancer in 1983, but the effort she put forth in memory of her husband continues to work toward finding a cure for HD.

The Guthrie and Wexler families provide an example of a psychological side effect of Huntington's disease. Huntington's is a genetic disease, so it runs in families. Woody Guthrie got it from his mother and passed it on to two of his children. We also know that a person who has a parent with a defective Huntington gene has a 50 percent chance of inheriting the disease. Symptoms of the disease often don't show up in a person until they are well into adulthood. By this time, they could already have children. These children then learn they have an even chance of having the disease, and they keep a fearful watch for the symptoms that will tell them they lost this genetic coin toss.

This constant fear is one of the topics written about by Alice Wexler, Leonore Wexler's other daughter, in her acclaimed book *Mapping Fate: A Memoir of Family, Risk, and Genetic Research.*

🧬 Breakthrough

Gillian Bates of King's College London develops the first HD mouse model in 1996. Bates finds aggregates, which are clumps of protein, in the brains of her mice. These aggregates are soon shown to be an important change found in HD patient brains.

GENETIC CARRIER

There are rare cases in which people inherit the defective Huntington gene from both parents. For these people, the symptoms of the disease are only slightly more severe than for people who inherit only one copy of the faulty gene. For those

Matt Austin (*left*), who was diagnosed with juvenile Huntington's disease, rode his bike 400 miles (644 kilometers) down the East Coast with his uncle Adam. Their journey was made into a documentary titled *Breaking the Cycle*.

who have two copies of the faulty gene, it is certain that they will pass the gene to their offspring.

When only one parent has the defective gene, having more than one child does not increase or decrease each child's risk. In some families, all the children might inherit the defective version of the Huntington gene. In others, maybe only one child inherits the gene. In still others, maybe no children inherit it.

THE START OF SYMPTOMS

While people with HD can start showing symptoms at any age, most people develop symptoms between the ages of thirty-five and fifty-five. Juvenile HD, also called early-onset HD, begins before the age of twenty.

For many people with HD, it is hard to figure out exactly when they began to develop symptoms. This is because the early symptoms of the disease can be very subtle, or not very noticeable. They can also vary widely from one person to the next. Many people may ignore symptoms because the changes are so gradual. For example, people may seem more forgetful than usual or have a slight twitch, but they may attribute this to something other than HD. This often happens if the person does not know he or she carries the faulty Huntington gene. For example, people who are adopted may not know the health history of their birth parents. Or people might not know they are at risk if a parent with HD died before showing symptoms or being diagnosed.

There are three distinct phases that people with Huntington's disease go through over the years, and they range from troublesome to disabling.

EARLY SYMPTOMS

The earliest and most common symptoms of both adult-onset and juvenile HD are usually related to mood and result in slight personality changes. For example, a person may seem edgier than usual. Some of these changes, such as increased moodiness and irritability, can be a result of frustration from dealing with other symptoms of the disease and may not actually be clinical symptoms.

Early physical signs include small involuntary movements. These movements may be mistaken for fidgeting during the early stages of the disease. They slowly become more noticeable as the disease progresses. Another early symptom is the loss of interest in personal hygiene. For example, the person may stop bathing, brushing his or her hair, or seeming to care about general appearance. Judgment and memory may also be affected. A person may have trouble driving, learning something new, remembering a fact, answering a question, or making a decision.

As the disease progresses further, other changes become more apparent. It may be harder for the person to concentrate. Trouble keeping balance and "clumsiness" may be more obvious as movement gets harder to control. Depression and mood swings, including anxiety and irritability, may also become more intense.

Many changes in behavior have been linked to HD. These include irritability, temper outbursts, and apathy. Apathy means not seeming to care about anything. HD patients may also seem to act in rude or thoughtless ways. These changes can affect relationships with family members and can cause problems at work.

Middle Stage Symptoms

During the middle stage of the disease, symptoms become more noticeable. Movement problems may make it challenging to do typical household chores, such as washing dishes and folding laundry. Muscle spasms, or uncontrolled movement, in the fingers, feet, face, trunk, and limbs also become more common.

Cristina Fuentes, who suffers from Huntington's disease, is assisted by her husband, Miguel, as she votes in 2010.

Changes in speech become more obvious. For example, the person suffering from HD may slur his or her words. Some people's speech may become hesitant, or halting. It may also become harder for the person to swallow. As the disease progresses, more nerve cells are destroyed, and patients increasingly lose control of their minds and bodies.

Studies show an increased rate of suicide in families with HD. For some patients, living with severe symptoms of HD—and knowing that HD is fatal—can make life feel unbearable.

Late Stage Symptoms

In the later stages of HD, severe movement disorders are common. These are due to increased neurological damage (damage to nerve cells in the brain). For many people, swallowing and speaking become almost impossible. Weight loss is common. This is a serious risk because it can lead to other health problems or weaken a person's ability to fight off illnesses.

People with adult-onset HD are more likely to experience chorea. For people who develop HD much later in life, the chorea tends to be more intense.

JUVENILE HD

Juvenile HD, or early-onset HD, is a form of Huntington's disease that affects children and teens. About 10 percent of people who have HD have this type. The biggest difference between juvenile HD and adult-onset HD is that many children do not experience chorea, a very common symptom of adult-onset HD.

In general, the earlier a person develops juvenile HD, the faster the disease appears to progress. How long each type of HD lasts is not significantly different, but juvenile HD tends to be slightly shorter. Early signs of juvenile HD may go unnoticed. Symptoms include feeling "growing pains" and having more and more trouble with schoolwork. Small changes in handwriting and speech, trouble learning new things, and small problems with movement are also symptoms. Common movement problems include slowness, clumsiness, tremors, or twitching. Children may also become less coordinated or tend to fall more often.

Sometimes diagnosing juvenile HD takes longer because the early symptoms are slightly different from those for adult-onset HD. For example, instead of the dancelike movements (chorea) common in adult HD, movements are stiff and rigid. Seizures are also a symptom in juvenile HD but uncommon in adult-onset HD patients. Also, if the person doesn't know he or she has a parent with HD, doctors may not link the symptoms to such a rare disease.

DIAGNOSING HD

Thanks to the discovery of the HD gene marker, it is now possible to perform DNA analysis to determine if a person is a carrier of the defective gene. This test is much more accurate than previous methods of testing and requires only a blood sample from the patient. The test can determine if a person has the defective gene before symptoms appear. However, the test cannot predict exactly when a person who has inherited the gene will begin to experience symptoms. In general, testing people who are under eighteen years old is not recommended. Exceptions might be made, however, if a child shows symptoms of juvenile HD.

Testing for HD, like testing for any serious disease, involves more than the procedure itself. Usually, testing for HD also involves counseling before and after the test. For people at risk of HD, deciding to find out if they carry the disease is a big decision. Testing is very personal. Some people want the test so that they know one way or the other and can make decisions about marriage, having children, their careers, and other long-

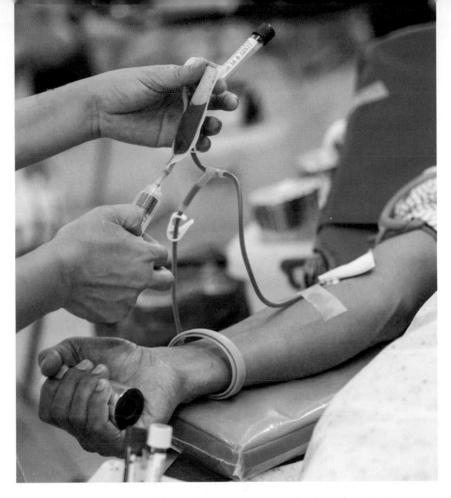

Testing for the presence of a defective Huntington gene can be done after collecting a blood sample.

term commitments. If they know, they can get treatment for symptoms as soon as they appear and have a better quality of life for a longer time.

Other people decide not to have the test because they are afraid they will change how they live their lives. The Wexler sisters chose not to know. They also chose not to have children who could inherit the disease. Both were still alive in 2015, and had lived past the age when Huntington's symptoms usually start to appear. Their father lived to be ninety-eight.

Chapter Four

Huntington's Disease Today

K elli Goodnight liked being a lawyer. When her hands went numb, and she began losing the ability to focus and to multitask she wanted to deny what she expected was true. Goodnight recognized the symptoms of Huntington's disease. She had seen the same things happen to her grandfather, her mother, and several uncles.

Doctors at the Indiana University School of Medicine confirmed her self-diagnosis, and they convinced her it was time to retire. "They talked me into treating the disease and focusing on being well," she told the *Kokomo Perspective* newspaper in June 2015. "It was hard to leave work. Even today, it's a part of my drive to do other things and help people. But it's frustrating to not be able to do it every day."

Meals high in calories help people fighting the advance of Huntington's disease maintain their weight.

Although there is no cure for HD, treatment can help make symptoms less severe. For example, antipsychotic drugs—medications usually used to treat severe mental disorders—may help suppress choreic movements. These same drugs may also help to reduce the hallucinations, delusions, or violent outbursts sometimes associated with HD. Antidepressant medications can be used to treat depression. For people who experience severe mood swings or anxiety, tranquilizers or lithium may be prescribed.

Unfortunately, many drugs used to treat HD symptoms have side effects, including tiredness and restlessness. These side effects can sometimes make it difficult to know if a behavior is a symptom of the disease or a side effect of a medication.

Nutrition also plays a role in treatment for HD. People with HD tend to burn a high number of calories from the constant involuntary movement caused by the disease. Keeping a healthy weight can help reduce involuntary movements and some other symptoms. A high-calorie diet can help people with HD stay at a healthy weight. In addition to maintaining a good diet, patients can learn to cope with symptoms of HD by working with physical, occupational, and speech therapists.

"If you are well rested and not stressed and take your vitamins and exercise, that helps it to be a better day," Goodnight told the newspaper. "The more stressed you get, the harder the emotional side is to control. When I was diagnosed, I was told I would have maybe five good years. That was ten years ago. I still have good days. For the most part I am hanging in there. Part of it is living carefully, eating and drinking and exercising carefully, taking supplements and vitamins. It has really helped."

Hard on Caregivers

Huntington's disease is not only hard for the person with it. Symptoms often don't show up until the person is married and a parent, leaving their care in the hands of an already busy spouse. Jerry D'Agostino and his wife, Shannon, also spoke to the *Kokomo Perspective* about their struggles with his condition.

"When we're going to a restaurant or a kid's event, his hands shake, and he has to constantly redirect himself," Shannon said to the reporter. "That is exhausting. Swaying, tipping, a lot of people think he's drunk ... There is no way to stay positive

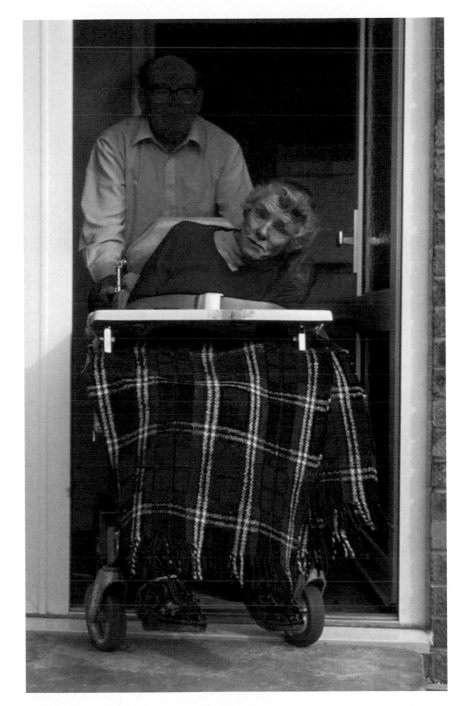

Caregivers need an occasional break from their duties so they can run errands or take part in activities that help them maintain their own health.

sometimes. You just have to regroup and go to bed and try to start fresh tomorrow. It's hard to do."

Caregivers face several huge challenges. One is learning to communicate with someone who has lost the ability to talk. Patients can regress physically and emotionally while maintaining their intellect, so frustration leading to bad behavior may set in. Eventually, the patient may develop dementia, which

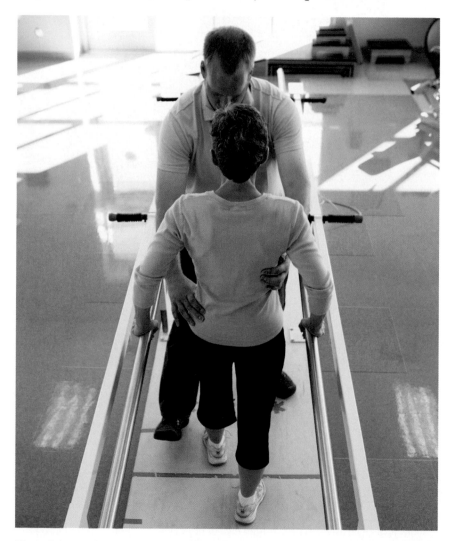

Physical therapists can help patients with Huntington's disease maintain their mobility.

Huntington's Disease

puts a whole new set of demands on loved ones. Help from family, friends, and neighbors can help caregivers take breaks to run errands or do things to maintain their own health.

Doctors can only treat the symptoms of Huntington's disease and not the condition itself. The goal is to improve the quality of life for the patient, and care is determined by the stage of the patient's condition. If a person is falling at home, for example, an occupational therapist may be called in to suggest changes to facilities in the house to make it more user-friendly for the patient. Then a physical therapist could help the patient maintain mobility.

If efforts to manage the condition without drugs fail, then tetrabenazine could be prescribed.

Breakthrough

Ai Yamamoto breeds an HD mouse in which the abnormal gene can be artificially switched off. In a 2000 study, switching off the gene allows mice that had already developed symptoms to get better.

Tetrabenazine, a drug used for the treatment of hyperkinetic movement disorder, reduces chorea. It is the only drug approved by the US Food and Drug Administration (FDA) for the treatment of HD. The patient should also be watched for depression and suicidal thoughts and given antidepressants if conditions make it necessary.

STILL SEEKING ANSWERS

Neurologists, psychologists, psychiatrists, and other scientists continue to study the symptoms and progression of HD in

Advancements in Huntington's Disease

• 1500s   The Renaissance physician and alchemist Paracelsus coins the term "chorea" to describe the dancelike movements now known to be symptoms of Huntington's disease.

• 1840s   HD is described in medical literature in the United States, England, and Norway.

• 1872   The landmark paper "On Chorea" is written by George Huntington. He bases his paper on personal accounts of his father's and grandfather's patients.

• 1910-   Researchers begin to note the deterioration of the
  1911   central region of the brain of HD patients. About this time, they also identify the caudate nucleus as the central target of brain cell death.

• 1976   Joseph T. Coyle develops the first rat model of HD.

• Late   Researchers discover evidence that HD affects cells
  1970s   throughout the body, not just in the brain.

• 1983   Scientists discover a gene marker linked to HD, which leads to locating the Huntington gene on chromosome 4. The discovery makes it possible to figure out if a person is likely to develop HD.

- 1993 Scientists more precisely locate the Huntington gene in February. This gene is called IT15 (interesting transcription 15). This discovery makes it possible to determine with even more certainty if a person will develop HD.

- 1996 Dr. Gillian P. Bates and her colleagues in London, England, create transgenic mouse models for HD research. The mice are genetically engineered to have nerve cell degeneration resembling Huntington's disease.

- 2003 Scientists involved in the Human Genome Project determine the sequence of all the nucleotides in the human genome.

- 2013 Alfred La Spada and other researchers at the University of California San Diego School of Medicine identify two proteins, PGC1-alpha and TFEB, that are vital to eliminating the proteins that cause Huntington's disease.

- 2014 Scientists at the Washington University School of Medicine convert skin cells into a type of brain cell affected by Huntington's disease. These converted brain cells, when transplanted into the brains of mice, survive at least six months and show properties similar to native **neurons.**

patients. They hope that by learning all they can, they will be able to develop new therapies. For example, positron emission tomography (PET) scans allow doctors to see how the defective gene affects various structures in the brain and how it affects the body's chemistry and **metabolism**. The more accurately scientists can predict how HD will affect the body, the more effectively they can treat symptoms and figure out how to slow or stop the disease from progressing.

Research has helped scientists gain a better understanding of Huntington's disease. An increased knowledge of genetics has contributed to a flurry of HD research advances in recent years. Most important was the discovery of the location of the Huntington gene. However, the exact function of the Huntington gene is a question researchers continue to struggle with today.

Until the day that question is answered, patients with Huntington's disease can only be comforted and not cured.

CHAPTER
FIVE

Long Way
to Go

Time is a very valuable commodity to people with the
Huntington's disease gene. If they are fully functional, they
know the day is coming soon when symptoms will indicate they
are losing brain function. If symptoms have flared, they know
that tomorrow can bring another setback. As a result, they try
to squeeze as much joy as they can into each day.

Charles Sabine is a former reporter for NBC television who
learned in 2005, at the age of forty-five, that he carried the gene
that has ravaged his father and his brother. He retired to a farm
in a rural area of the United Kingdom, but he has advocated
genetic testing. He is excited about advancements in HD
research but is realistic about his future.

"I think they're too late for me," he said to a *Washington Post*
reporter in 2013, in reference to treatments being developed.

Charles Sabine retired from his job as a television news reporter after coming down with the disease that has ravaged his family.

"But the next generation has every reason to believe that they do not have to fear this disease as much as I do."

PROTEIN TRIGGERS

Researchers share Sabine's optimism, but caution that treatments could be decades away. They have made great headway in learning how the Huntington's genetic mutation causes the deterioration of the brain. They have also found ways to slow down or reverse the effects of the disease in mice and other animal models.

Huntington's Disease

However, they have not tested any of their treatments on humans, so there is no guarantee that any will lead to a cure.

The treatments include introducing agents into the body to counter the effects of the huntingtin protein, performing gene therapy, and prescribing medicine that can halt or slow the course of the disease.

Finding a cure for HD involves studying how the abnormal huntingtin protein produced in HD causes the disease. The abnormal huntingtin protein activates a team of enzymes in a cell that awaken a regulatory protein called factor p53. This protein normally helps protect the cell, keeping it whole and functioning. When p53 detects damaged DNA in a cell, it can tell the cell to commit suicide for the good of the entire organism. This is the way factor p53 acts as a tumor suppressor; it can tell damaged cells to commit suicide before they can reproduce and turn into cancerous tumors.

At the Johns Hopkins University School of Medicine, a study led by Akira Sawa showed that the abnormal huntingtin protein binds to p53 and then increases the level of p53 proteins in cells. In brains of patients with HD, there were substantial increases in the p53 protein. The highest levels were in cases with the most advanced HD. Increased amounts of p53 causes damage to mitochondria, which are

Breakthrough

Doctors perform gene silencing tests on monkeys at three sites in 2011 and find that the drugs injected into the animals' brains reached the targets and did no damage. The goal is to tell cells to stop making the protein that causes HD.

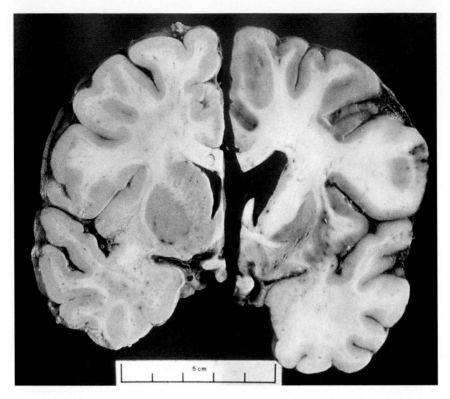

Two human hemispheres of a human brain illustrate the difference between a healthy brain (*left*) and one damaged by Huntington's disease. Protein aggregates have caused cell death. The large, open area in the middle of the right hemisphere shows the loss of cells in the basal ganglia. The dark brown area (*top right*) shows damage to the cortex.

organelles, or specialized parts, inside a cell. Mitochondria are like a cell's power plant; they are the main energy source of the cell. They also convert nutrients into energy and do other special tasks. When the mitochondria in brain cells don't function properly, the brain cells are damaged and can die.

Researchers found that if they deleted p53, they could prevent damage to neurons in the eyes of fruit flies that had been engineered to have the abnormal huntingtin protein. They then tested the theory in mice. When they removed p53, behavioral abnormalities associated with HD were corrected in the mice.

Huntington's Disease

The engine that balances the use of energy in a cell is the mammalian target of rapamycin complex 1, or mTORC1. Activity in the network regulated by mTORC1 is reduced in HD patients. Researchers used a virus to deliver a powerful signal that would turn on the brains of mice and artificially increase activity. When this was done, areas of the brain that had started to shrink recovered, movement was improved, and the cells were able to clean out mutant huntingtin.

The big problem to be overcome is ensuring the proper balance of energy so no harm is done. Too much energy can cause problems; autism is linked to too much mTORC1 activity.

Albert La Spada, who found the original genetic stutter that causes HD, made another huge breakthrough. A story published by *Medical News Today* early in 2014 said that La Spada and his fellow researchers at the University of California San Diego School of Medicine had found two regulatory proteins that are vital to eliminating the misfolding of the huntingtin proteins into the aggregates that cause HD. These regulatory proteins are called PGC1-alpha and TFEB. In a mouse model, elevated levels of PGC1-alpha got rid of the HD-causing proteins. TFEB can stop Htt aggregation and the resulting death of brain cells.

"Degeneration of brain cells is prevented. Neurons don't die," La Spada said in the *Medical News Today* article. He added that increasing TFEB function could stop the disease process before it gets started.

There are other reasons for optimism. Some researchers have attempted to replace neurons lost to Huntington's disease with new ones with a surgery known as fetal neural transplantation. This procedure has been attempted on very few people. It gave some of them several years of improvement and stability, but the

Family Doctor

Dr. Victor McKusick was trained as a cardiologist, but he would make his mark in another medical discipline. His life's work took a turn when he treated a tall patient with a weakening of the aorta

Victor A. McKusick receives the Japan Award in 2008 for his work in identifying and mapping genes that cause inherited diseases.

and a detached retina. The patient had a rare inherited disease called Marfan syndrome, which is marked by features such as abnormal height, heart defects, and long fingers with round nails.

Sought out by other Marfan patients, he began keeping records of the inheritance patterns and features of the syndrome. Soon, he was studying relatively isolated populations, such as the Amish in Pennsylvania, using their histories to identify genes responsible for their inherited disorders.

His list of advances in genetics is long. He led a team that mapped a gene for a blood group on chromosome 1 in 1968. No one had ever identified a gene on a non-sex chromosome. He established a database of gene functions; it included eighteen thousand genes at the time of his death in 2008. He is most famous for cofounding the Short Course in Medical and Experimental Mammalian Genetics at the Jackson Laboratory in Bar Harbor, Maine. Thousands of doctors and researchers have studied there. He was an early proponent of mapping the human genome. He was also among the first to recognize the value of using mice as a model for human diseases, a method that has proven indispensible to Huntington's disease research. In 1991, he located the gene responsible for Marfan syndrome.

His name is attached to the McKusick-Nathans Institute of Genetic Medicine at Johns Hopkins University School of Medicine, where he spent most of his career. He is known as the Father of Medical Genetics.

improvement faded four to six years after the surgery. There were side effects, and not all patients benefitted from the new cells.

Patients with HD and Parkinson's disease may have an excessive amount of enzymes called **transglutaminases**. A transglutaminase inhibitor—something that inhibits the actions of these enzymes—called cystamine was given to mouse models after the appearance of abnormal movements, and it extended survival, reduced tremor and abnormal movements, and helped patients maintain weight.

REVERSING HD SYMPTOMS

At the Columbia University College of Physicians and Surgeons, researchers use mouse models to study diseases like HD that lead to the loss or damage of nerve cells. Doctors René Hen and Ai Yamamoto genetically engineered mice so they could experiment with turning a defective Huntington gene on and off. They did this by fusing the defective gene to a promoter that they could regulate. A promoter is a piece of DNA that does not code for a protein. Instead, it controls the expression of a particular gene, in this case, the Huntington gene. They were able to "turn off" the faulty gene by giving the mice a diet that included tetracycline, an antibiotic drug used to treat infections.

When the mice with the inserted gene were given a regular diet, the gene was expressed, and cells produced the defective form of the huntingtin protein. Soon the mice began showing signs of HD. When tetracycline was added to the diet, however, the symptoms of HD lessened. This suggests that when the gene was "turned off," the brain was able to cure itself. The movements of the mice improved, as did their memory and overall condition. These results provided the first hope that HD could be reversed.

Another group of researchers, led by Beverly Davidson of the University of Iowa, also discovered new ways of "turning off" the HD gene and still leaving the normal protein intact and able to function. This process is called RNA (ribonucleic acid) interference, or RNAi.

RNAi is different from conventional gene therapy because it specifically targets the defective Huntington gene. Conventional gene therapy works by adding a normal gene. It is useful when a disorder is caused by a recessive gene, meaning the affected person has two copies of the disease gene. In conventional therapy, a normal gene is added, and because the normal gene is dominant, it will take over.

However, with HD (and some other genetic disorders), the disease gene is dominant. In this case, conventional gene therapy will not work. As long as the defective Huntington gene exists in the cell, the huntingtin protein will be produced with too many glutamines. The strategy in this situation is to disrupt the expression of the disease gene.

RNAi suppresses the defective gene but leaves the healthy version of the same gene to carry out its duties. This method, called gene silencing, was the first of its kind to have successful results in the brains of animals. Researchers have yet to find a way to disrupt the defective Huntington gene in humans without also disrupting the function of the normal Huntington gene. Researchers are also trying to develop RNAi that can be turned off with the antibiotic tetracycline.

Two other antibiotic drugs have been shown to be effective in slowing the progression of the disease. Tests showed that

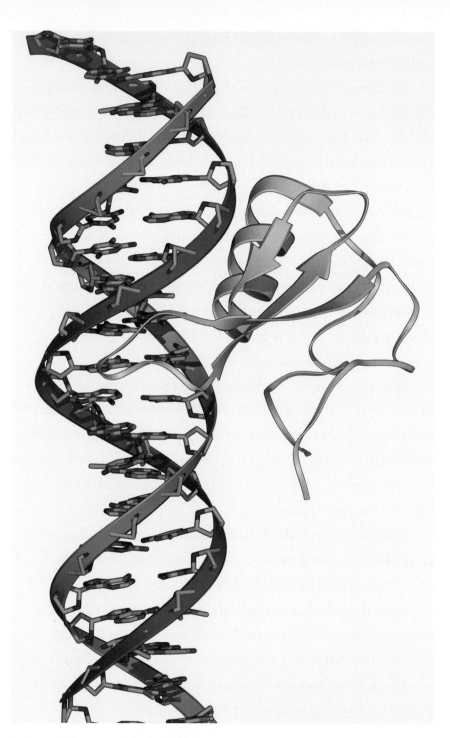

In this model, a protein binds to DNA so it can silence a mutated gene.

Huntington's Disease

rapamycin appeared to delay the onset of HD in cell, fly, and mouse models. The medicine reduced the levels of the toxic protein that causes HD. The drug worked by speeding up the breakdown of the protein in cells. Rapamycin targets mTORC1.

Another medicine that may eventually prove effective in humans is mithramycin. Researchers have found that mithramycin greatly slows the breakdown of nerve cells in the brains of HD mouse models. This lessens the severity of HD symptoms and allows the mice to live longer.

Researchers are also learning to use new tools to edit genes. These tools are bacterial weapons that can cut genes in targeted places, and they have exotic names such as zinc finger nucleases (ZFNs) and Clustered Regularly Interspaced Short Palindromic Repeats (CRISPR).

Huntington's disease is caused by a stutter that creates extra copies of the C-A-G repeat. The idea with gene editing is to cut out the extra copies so the gene functions properly, or to remove part of the mutant HD gene so its code never produces a protein. The editing has worked in mice, but there is still concern over the accuracy of the targeting. There is no guarantee the editing tools won't cut out something that is healthy and necessary. Until that problem and other problems are solved, there won't be any testing in humans.

The National Institutes of Health concluded that while these developments show promise, some lab breakthroughs have been unsuccessful in humans for unknown reasons. It is not known if one approach is better than the others because many have not been tested in humans. Therefore, all options for treatment should be explored.

aggregate • A biological phenomenon in which misfolded proteins clump together and disrupt the normal function of cells, which can result in cell death.

alchemist • One who studied the medieval science of transforming base metals, such as iron, into gold.

caudate nucleus • The central target in the brain of brain cell death in patients with HD. It affects movement and behavior.

chorea • A neurological disorder marked by uncontrollable body movement, especially of the shoulders, hips, and face.

chromosome • A bundle of DNA and protein found in the cell nucleus. Except for the sex cells, normal human cells have forty-six chromosomes (twenty-three pairs).

cortex • The outer layer of an organ, such as the brain, or other body structure.

degenerative • Causing gradual deterioration, or making less healthy over time.

DNA (deoxyribonucleic acid) • The chemical structure for genetic material. DNA is made up of four types of nucleic acid: adenine, thymine, cytosine, and guanine (or A, T, C, and G). These are the letters of the genetic code.

dominant • A gene from a pair that will be expressed. A recessive gene will not be expressed unless a child inherits one from each parent.

enzyme • A protein produced by a living organism that kicks off a specific biochemical reaction.

ganglia • Clusters of neurons located outside the central nervous system. Basal ganglia are involved in the coordination of movement.

genetic • Determined by genes; inherited.

genetic mutation • A permanent alteration of the DNA sequence that makes up a gene.

genome • An organism's complete set of DNA.

glutamine • A building block of protein. The huntingtin protein contains a series of glutamine building blocks. Glutamine is an amino acid.

hereditary • Passed from parent to child through genes.

huntingtin • The protein that is coded by the Huntington gene. Normal huntingtin proteins have a repeat series of up to thirty-six glutamines. Abnormal huntingtin has more than forty glutamine repeats.

metabolism • The chemical changes in living cells related to the production of energy and the assimilation of new material.

neurology • The study of the nervous system.

neurons • Cells that make up the central nervous system. The human brain is made up of billions of neurons.

nucleotide • The basic building block of nucleic acids, such as DNA and RNA.

proteins • Chemicals that make up the structure of cells.

transglutaminase • A clotting factor that is a variant of factor XIII and that promotes the formation of cross-links between strands of fibrin. This may contribute to aggregates.

Websites

Genetics Home Reference: Huntington's Disease

ghr.nlm.nih.gov/condition/huntington-disease

This guide to genetic conditions provides a concise definition of the disease and multiple links to other resources.

HOPES

web.stanford.edu/group/hopes/cgi-bin/hopes_test/

The Huntington's Outreach Project for Education, at Stanford, is a multimedia, student-run project at Stanford University that provides comprehensive information about the disease and its treatments.

NINDS Huntington's Disease Information Page

www.ninds.nih.gov/disorders/huntington/huntington.htm

The National Institute of Neurological Disorders and Stroke, a division of the National Institutes of Health, collects news and information about Huntington's disease.

Organizations

Hereditary Disease Foundation
3690 Broadway, Sixth Floor
New York, NY 10032
(212) 928-2121
www.hdfoundation.org

Huntington's Disease Association
Suite 24, Liverpool Science Park IC1
131 Mount Pleasant
Liverpool L3 5TF
United Kingdom
www.hda.org.uk

**Huntington's Disease
Society of America**
505 Eighth Avenue, Suite 902
New York, NY 10018
(212) 242-1968
www.hdsa.org

For Further Reading

Barema, Jean. *The Test: Living in the Shadow of Huntington's Disease*. New York: Franklin Square Press, 2010.

Glimm, Adele. *Gene Hunter: The Story of Neuropsychologist Nancy Wexler*. Women's Adventures in Science. Washington, DC: Joseph Henry Press, 2006.

Lawrence, Susan E. *All Within: The Internal Journey of Huntington's Disease*. Frederick, MD: America Star Books, 2012.

Naff, Clayton Farris, ed. *Huntington's Disease*. Perspectives on Diseases and Disorders. Farmington Hills, MI: Greenhaven Press, 2012.

Partridge, Elizabeth. *This Land Was Made for You and Me: The Life and Songs of Woody Guthrie*. New York: Viking, 2002.

Sulaiman, Sandy. *Learning to Live With Huntington's Disease: One Family's Story*. London: Jessica Kingsley Publishers, 2007.

Thompson, Michelle Hardt. *Afraid: A Book for Children "At Risk" for Huntington's Disease*. Glendale, AZ: Huntington's Disease Society of America, Arizona Chapter, 2002.

Wexler, Alice. *Mapping Fate: A Memoir of Family, Risk, and Genetic Research*. Oakland, CA: University of California Press, 1996.

Wexler, Alice. *The Woman Who Walked Into the Sea: Huntington's and the Making of a Genetic Disease*. New Haven, CT: Yale University Press, 2008.

Selected Bibliography

Publications

Parker, James N., and Philip M. Parker. *The Official Patient's Sourcebook on Huntington's Disease*. San Diego, CA: ICON Group International Inc., 2002.

Partridge, Elizabeth. *This Land Was Made for You and Me: The Life and Songs of Woody Guthrie*. New York: Viking, 2002.

Quarrell, Oliver. *Huntington's Disease: The Facts*. New York: Oxford University Press, 2008.

Online Articles

Brown, David. "Former TV Reporter Campaigns to Bring Huntington's Disease Out of the Shadows." *Washington Post*. July 29, 2013. Retrieved June 5, 2015. www.washingtonpost.com/national/health-science/former-tv-reporter-campaigns-to-bring-huntingtons-disease-out-of-the-shadows/2013/07/29/136d1a9e-bd70-11e2-9b09-1638acc3942e_story.html

Cha, Jang-Ho J., and Anne B. Young. "Huntington's Disease." The American College of Neuropsychopharmacology. Retrieved June 23, 2015. www.acnp.org/g4/gn401000151/ch.html

Frazin, Natalie. "Silencing Gene Activity Prevents Disease in Model for
Huntington's." National Institute of Neurological Disorders and Stroke.
June 7, 2005. Retrieved June 23, 2015. www.ninds.nih.gov/news_and_
events/news_articles/news_article_Huntington_RNAi.htm

Kokomo Perspective. "Seeking Support: Huntington's Sufferers Form
Group to Educate, Comfort." Kokomo Perspective. June 10, 2015.
Retrieved June 12, 2015. kokomoperspective.com/kp/seeking-support/
article_30529aaa-0eb6-11e5-8c4e-63ca4c48e746.html

Liu, Stephanie. "Huntington Protein and Protein Aggregation." HOPES.
February 5, 2011. Retrieved June 1, 2015. web.stanford.edu/group/
hopes/cgi-bin/hopes_test/huntingtin-protein-and-protein-aggregation/

Mayo Clinic Staff. "Huntington's Disease." Mayo Clinic. Retrieved June 23,
2015. www.mayoclinic.com/invoke.cfm?id=DS00401&dsection=1

Rattue, Grace. "Two Proteins Identified That May Offer 'Clearer' Way to
Treat Huntington's Disease." Medical News Today. January 8, 2014.
Retrieved June 23, 2015. www.medicalnewstoday.com/articles/247972.php

Wild, Dr. Ed. "Interview: Alice and Nancy Wexler." HDBuzz. October 20,
2012. Retrieved June 23, 2015. en.hdbuzz.net/101

Wild, Dr. Ed. "Safety Trials Add Crucial Piece to Gene Silencing." HDBuzz.
November 11, 2011. Retrieved July 1, 2011. en.hdbuzz.net/058

INDEX

Page numbers in **boldface** are illustrations. Entries in **boldface** are glossary terms.